Date Due

LET'S INVESTIGATE SCIENCE
Matter and Materials

LET'S INVESTIGATE SCIENCE

Matter and Materials

Robin Kerrod

Illustrated by Terry Hadler

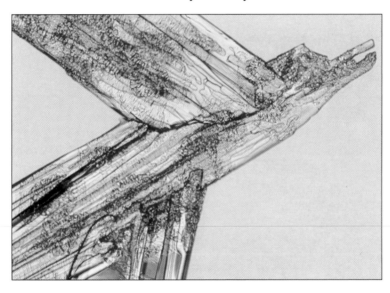

BENCHMARK BOOKS

MARSHALL CAVENDISH
NEW YORK

Library Edition Published 1996

Benchmark Books
Marshall Cavendish Corporation
99 White Plains Road
Tarrytown, New York 10591

© Marshall Cavendish Corporation 1996

Series created by Graham Beehag Books

Library of Congress Cataloging-in-Publication Data

Kerrod, Robin.
    Matter and Materials / Robin Kerrod; illustrated by Terry Hadler,
      p. cm. – (Lets investigate science)
    Includes bibliographical references and index.
    Summary: Dicsusses the nature and states of matter and examines both natural and synthetic materials such as forest products, rocks, minerals, and metals.
    ISBN 0-7614-0031-1 (lib. bdg.)
    1. Matter – Properties – Juvenile literature. 2. Materials – Juvenile literature. [1. Matter. 2. Materials.]
    I. Hadler, Terry, ill. II. Title. III. Series: Kerrod, Robin. Let's investigate science.
    QC173.36.K47 1995
    530–dc20
                             95-16530
                                CIP
                                AC

Printed in Hong Kong

Contents

Introduction

Everything that exists is made up of the stuff we call matter. The rocks that make up the Earth, the water that flows in the rivers, the air that we breathe, and the stars in the sky: all these things are different kinds of matter. The whole Universe is made up of matter, distributed throughout space.

All the many different forms of matter are made up of a relatively small number of basic "building blocks," which we call the elements. The elements combine together in different ways to create the various materials – different forms of matter – we are familiar with.

The study of the elements – their properties, the way they combine, and the compounds they form, is one of the main branches of science. It is called chemistry.

In the first two chapters of this book, we investigate the general properties of matter and the different states in which it is found. We look at the chemical elements, and at the way they react together to create a multitude of different kinds of substances. In the third chapter, we look at the most important raw materials we use and how we process them to make the goods we buy.

You can check your answers to the questions, investigations, and workouts featured throughout this book on pages 60-62.

◀ Cars crossing a suspension bridge. The bridge and the cars are made from our most useful material of construction, steel. The supporting towers are built on massive foundations of concrete, a rock-hard mixture of cement, gravel, and stone chips. In the bridge design, the properties of steel and concrete combine to make a strong, safe structure.

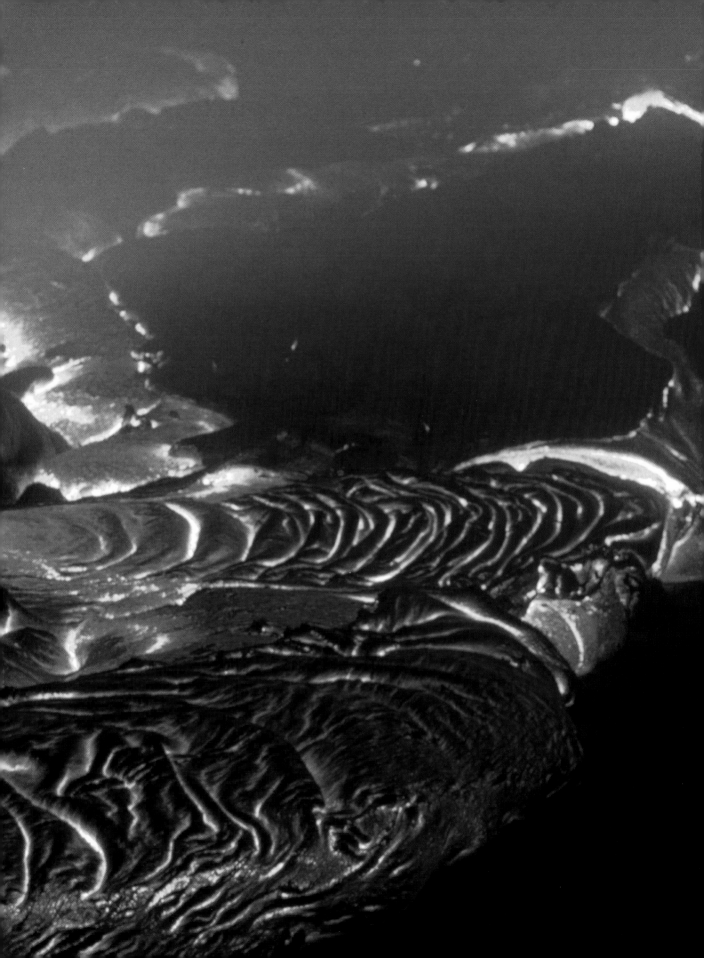

1
States of Matter

◀ A volcano pouring out rivers of molten lava. Lava is rock in the form of a liquid. The rock melted when it was heated deep down in the Earth's crust. Now that the lava is flowing on the surface, it will soon cool and become solid again. Most substances change their state if they are heated or cooled enough.

▼ A beautiful sunrise viewed from Earth orbit by shuttle astronauts. The layer of air around the Earth is clearly defined. Air represents matter in its gaseous form.

What is the main difference between steel, water, and air? The main difference lies in their physical form, or state. Steel represents matter in its solid state. Water represents matter in its liquid state, and air represents matter in its gaseous state. On Earth, all matter exists in one of these three states. They are called the three states of matter.

A substance does not exist in just one state under all conditions. If the temperature changes, for example, a substance can change its state. Water is one substance that readily changes its state. On a very cold night, the water in a puddle changes state. It becomes a solid – ice. On a hot day, on the other hand, the water in a puddle disappears. It changes into a gas – water vapor – and escapes into the air.

Q On a shuttle mission, the astronauts see 16 sunrises a day. Why is this?

IT'S AMAZING!

The particles of a gas whiz about at an average speed of about 1,000 mph (1,600 km/h). They bump into other particles about 10 billion times every second.

The kinetic theory

We shall see in this chapter how solids, liquids, and gases behave differently from one another. We shall also see that they can change their state when the temperature changes. How can we explain their behavior?

We can explain it by supposing that all matter is made up of tiny particles, and that these particles move in some way. They move faster as the temperature rises. This basic idea about matter is called the kinetic theory. The word "kinetic" comes from a Greek word meaning "movement."

Rigid solids

In a substance in the solid state, the particles are close together and forces between the particles bind them tightly. The particles vibrate slightly, but can't break free from one another. They form a rigid structure. Usually, in this structure the particles are arranged in a regular pattern, or lattice. Such regular patterns give rise to the shapes of crystals.

▼ **Most substances can exist as solids, liquids, and gases at different temperatures. These diagrams show how the structure of a substance changes as the substance changes from a solid to a liquid to a gas.**

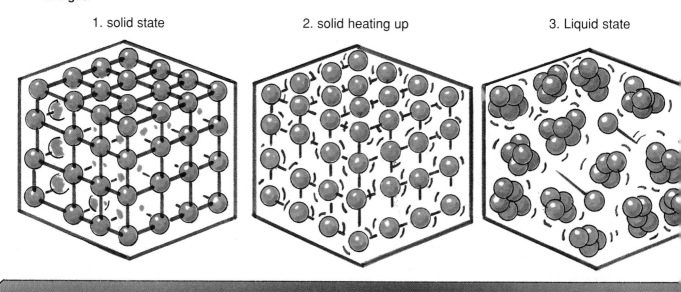

1. solid state   2. solid heating up   3. Liquid state

Flowing liquids

When a solid substance is heated, its particles vibrate more vigorously. Eventually, as heating continues, little clumps of particles start moving fast enough to break free from one another. The solid changes into a liquid.

Speeding gases

As the temperature rises further, the particles in the clumps forming the liquid move faster. Some gain enough energy to break out of the clumps and escape from the liquid surface as a gas. The escaped particles shoot about freely, leading an independent existence. As the temperature continues to rise, more and more particles escape.

4. Gaseous state

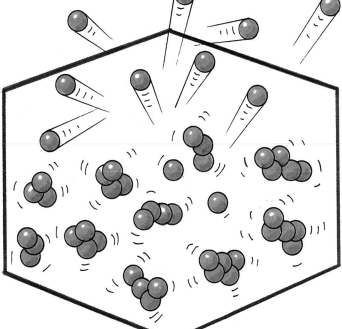

WORKOUT

Using its feathery antennae, a male moth picks up the scent of a female moth 3,000 yards (2,700 meters) away. How long would it take for the male moth to reach the female from the instant she sends out her scent particles? Assume that a scent particle can travel as fast as an ordinary gas particle, and that a moth can fly at a speed of 7 mph (11 km/h).

Below: **The crystals in granite are clearly visible.**

Bottom: **A beautiful iceberg floating near Ellesmere Island in the Arctic. Strangely, ice (water in the solid state) is less dense than water in the liquid state. Most substances in their solid state are denser than they are in their liquid state.**

The solid state

Most of the substances we come across in our everyday lives are solid. A piece of rock is a typical solid. It is hard and has a definite size and shape. No matter how hard you squeeze it, you can't change its shape.

The kinetic theory explains these properties: the particles in a solid attract one another strongly and bind together to form a rigid structure.

Mineral crystals

Many rocks, such as granite, are made up of many colored glassy bits mixed together. These bits are crystals of the substances of which the rock is made up. These substances are called minerals.

In most rocks, the crystals of the various minerals have grown together to form a solid mass, and they have no particular shape. In some rocks, however, the crystals have formed in holes. They have been able to grow unhindered, and have made beautifully shaped crystals.

No matter where it is found, each mineral grows crystals of the same shape. Crystals of the most common mineral, quartz, for example, are always found in the form of

pointed six-sided fingers, while crystals of fluorite are always cubes.

A great many solids, in fact, form crystals, although they can't always be seen. Even metals form crystals. You can often see feathery crystals on the surface of a galvanized bucket. This bucket is made of steel coated with a very thin layer of zinc. The feathery crystals are of zinc.

Q 1. What is the purpose of coating the steel with zinc?

Crystal structures

Hundreds of substances form crystals, but there are not hundreds of different crystal shapes. Crystals can be divided into six or seven basic families, or systems, according to their shape. There are also variations within each family.

There is a good reason why a substance forms a crystal with a particular shape. This shape tells us the way in which the particles that make up the substance are put together.

For example, if the crystal is a cube, the particles are arranged like this:

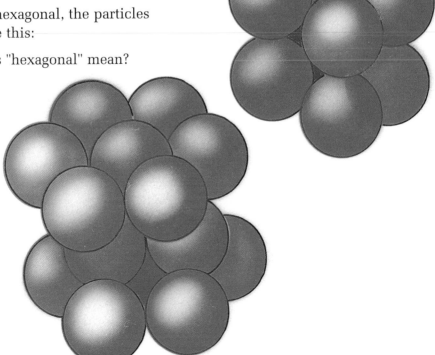

Microscope views of magnesium sulfate crystals (top) and chloral hydrate (above).

If the crystal is hexagonal, the particles are arranged like this:

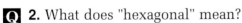

Q 2. What does "hexagonal" mean?

Water tumbles over the rocks as it flows downward under gravity.

Q In some places, we harness the power in flowing water to make electricity. What do we call electricity made in this way?

The liquid state

The most common liquid on Earth is water. In fact, the water in the oceans covers over 70 percent of the Earth's surface. Our experience with water tells us much about the general properties of a liquid. Water flows when you pour it out of a bottle. It flows downward under the action of gravity. When you pour water into a glass, it settles in the bottom of the glass and takes the shape of the glass.

Summing up, liquids flow – they are fluids. They have a definite size, but no definite shape. They take the shape of any container they are poured into.

The kinetic theory explains that liquids are made up of little bundles of particles moving about. The force of attraction between the bundles is less than the force of gravity. Therefore they move downhill: in other words, they flow.

Surface tension

The bundles of particles moving about in the middle of a liquid are attracted in all directions to other bundles, including up and down. However, the bundles at the surface are attracted only by bundles from the sides and underneath because there are no bundles above them. This results in a skin-like effect at the surface, as these tiny bundles tug on each other. We call it surface tension.

If you look carefully at the surface of a pond, you will see tiny insects and bits of dust making little dents in this skin. Some creatures actually walk on this skin, including the well-named water strider or pond skater.

INVESTIGATE

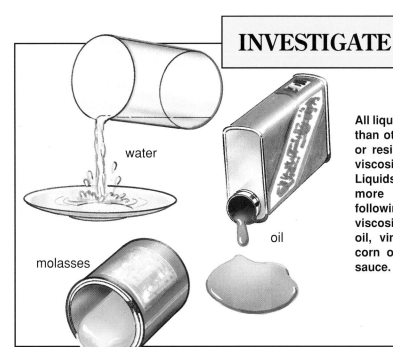

water

oil

molasses

Liquids in motion

All liquids flow, but some flow more readily than others. It depends on their viscosity, or resistance to flow. Liquids with a low viscosity flow easily when they are poured. Liquids with a high viscosity flow much more slowly. By experiment, list the following liquids in order of increasing viscosity: dishwashing liquid, water, olive oil, vinegar, tomato ketchup, motor oil, corn oil, cola, molasses, milk, barbecue sauce.

Some of the beautiful stained glass in Chartres Cathedral, France. Glass looks like a solid crystal. In fact, it isn't. It has no regular structure. It is really a liquid that has been supercooled. We could call it a solid liquid.

INVESTIGATE

Floating needles

Steel doesn't float, does it? Yes it does! You can make it float. Take a clean bowl and wash it thoroughly several times and fill it with water. Wash your hands thoroughly and rinse them several times, then dry them. Take a clean, dry paper clip between finger and thumb and place it gently on the surface of the water. Carefully remove your fingers, and the paper clip should stay afloat. If you fail the first time, try again. You should eventually be able to make the paper clip float. It floats on the "skin" on the surface of the water. When you have succeeded in making the paper clip float, add a drop of dishwashing liquid to the water. What happens?

The gaseous state

We are surrounded by, and breathe in and out, matter in its third state – gas. The general properties of air are much like those of other gases.

Air is invisible, so how do we know it's there? We can feel it when the wind blows. Wind is air in motion. Most other gases are invisible. We can sense them only when they move or when they have an odor. One of the smelliest gases is hydrogen sulfide, which has the odor of rotten eggs. A few gases are colored. Chlorine is one of them, being greenish-yellow. It also has a distinctive smell and is poisonous.

A gas has no particular shape. It fills any container completely. It has no particular size either. You can compress gas – force it into a smaller space by increasing the pressure on it. You can't compress solids in this way.

The kinetic theory tells us that the particles in a gas travel about independently and at very high speeds. Compared with liquids and solids, the gas particles have plenty of space to travel in. Because they travel fast, they quickly fill any container they are put into.

When you blow up a tire, you force more air into the tire.

Q 1. Fill in the missing word here: The tire gets harder as you force more air into it; its _ _ _ _ _ _ _ _ increases.

Q 2. The valve on the tire gets hotter as you pump in the air. Why?

▶ Sailboats catch the wind in their large sails.

Q 3. On a good sailing day, the wind may blow at a speed of 30 mph (50 km/h). Yet a sailboat will travel only about half this speed. What is keeping the boat from moving faster?

Gas laws

The particles of gas striking the walls of a container exert pressure on that container. As the temperature rises, the particles travel faster. If they remain in the same container, that is, in the same volume, they will strike the walls harder. In other words, the pressure in the container will increase.

If on the other hand the container is flexible, the faster gas particles may make it expand, or increase its volume.

Also in your flexible container, if you squeeze the gas into a smaller space, more particles will strike a given area of wall. Thus, the pressure on that wall will increase.

Thus, we can see that the pressure (P), volume (V), and temperature (T) of a gas are closely related. The relationship between them can be summed up by the equation:

$$PV = RT, \text{ where R is a constant}$$

This relationship is called the equation of state.

INVESTIGATE

Smoking bottles

Fill a jar with smoke from a snuffed-out candle. Join the jar mouth to mouth with another, using a rubber ring as a seal. What happens to the smoke? Does it stay in the one jar? Repeat the experiment placing the smoke-filled jar first on top of, and then underneath the second jar. What happens now?

▶ A remote galaxy, made up of billions of stars. In these and all other stars, including our Sun, matter exists in a form not found on Earth. It is so hot in the stars that matter splits up, forming a kind of substance called a plasma. Plasma is often called the fourth state of matter.

INVESTIGATE

Place a handful of ice cubes in a saucepan and add a little water. Take the temperature of the water. You will find it is 32°F (0°C). Put the saucepan on a low heat and keep taking the temperature of the water until the last ice cube has melted. Does the temperature of the water start rising as soon as you start heating the saucepan?

Changing state

If you place some ice cubes in a saucepan and heat them, they turn into liquid water. If you continue heating the water, it will start steaming and bubbling and gradually disappear. It will change into water vapor, a gas.

When most solids are heated strongly enough, they turn into liquids. When liquids are heated, they turn into gases. The opposite also applies. When you cool gases enough, they turn back to liquids. When you cool liquids enough, they turn back into solids.

In other words, a large enough change in temperature brings about a change in state of a substance. The kinetic theory tells us how these changes of state occur.

Melting

A solid turns into a liquid when its particles gain enough energy to break the rigid bonds between them. They form bundles of particles, which can move about.

This change of state from solid to liquid is called melting. For a given substance under the same conditions, melting always takes place at the same temperature – the melting point. The melting points of substances vary widely. Mercury melts at a temperature of about −38°F (−39°C). Ice melts at a temperature of 32°F (0°C). Iron melts at a temperature of 2,795°F (1,535°C).

Q Mercury is a metal. Why is it special?

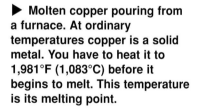

▶ **Molten copper pouring from a furnace. At ordinary temperatures copper is a solid metal. You have to heat it to 1,981°F (1,083°C) before it begins to melt. This temperature is its melting point.**

Freezing

Liquids turn back into solids, a change of state known as freezing. A liquid substance always freezes at the same temperature, the freezing point. For a given substance, the freezing point of the substance in the liquid state is exactly the same temperature as the melting point of the solid state.

Evaporation

When you heat a liquid, its particles gain energy. At any time, some may gain enough energy to escape from the surface of the liquid and form a gas. This change of state from liquid to gas is called evaporation. The boiling occurs more rapidly as the temperature rises.

At a certain temperature, all the particles have gained enough energy to escape. The liquid bubbles violently and almost explodes into gas – it boils. This temperature is called the boiling point. Again, for a given substance under the same conditions, the boiling point is always the same. The boiling point of pure water at sea level is 212°F (100°C).

▲ Here, up in the mountains, moisture in the air has cooled and condensed into fine droplets. It has formed low clouds that cling to the rugged mountainside.

Condensation

When a substance in a gaseous state is cooled to the boiling point of the substance in its liquid state, the gas turns back into liquid. We say it condenses.

Evaporation and condensation play an essential part in our weather. Water is evaporating from the surface all the time, turning into water vapor in the air. In the air, the vapor cools and condenses, forming mists and clouds.

20

Solutions

When you add a spoonful of sugar to your cup of tea and stir it, the sugar disappears. When you sip the tea, you find that it is sweet, so the sugar is still there. We say it has dissolved in the water in the cup to form a sugar solution. The tiny particles that make up the sugar have mixed thoroughly with the particles that make up the water.

In this solution, sugar is known as the solute, and water is the solvent. Water dissolves many other substances, such as table salt, bath salts, and baking soda. There are also many substances that do not dissolve in water. Sand and glass are examples. We say these substances are insoluble in water.

Dissolving liquids

Water may also dissolve other liquids. It dissolves alcohol, for example. Wines and spirits are solutions of alcohol in water. Liquids that dissolve in one another are called miscible liquids. Many liquids do not dissolve in one another. Oil and water are examples. We say these liquids are immiscible.

Q Why can't you put out an oil fire with water?

▲ A diver swims with colorful angel fish and sergeant majors. The fish breathe by using the oxygen dissolved in the water. The diver, however, has to carry his oxygen with him in an air tank.

INVESTIGATE

Stirring it up

Pour some water from the cold tap into a glass and add salt to it gradually, using a small spoon. Count the number of spoonfuls you add. Each time, stir the solution until the salt disappears. After a certain number of spoonfuls, you will find that the salt won't dissolve any more. The salt solution has become saturated.

Repeat the experiment using (A) water you have cooled in an ice bucket and (B) water from the hot tap.

Does the temperature of the water affect how much salt you can add before the solution becomes saturated? Now repeat the experiment using sugar. Do you get similar results?

Dissolving gases

Water does not dissolve only solids and liquids, it also dissolves gases. It is just as well that it does, because otherwise we couldn't live. We breathe by taking in oxygen from the air. In our lungs, the oxygen dissolves in our blood, which is mostly water. The blood carries the oxygen all around the body to take part in the energy-producing processes that keep us alive.

We can see how water dissolves gases when we open a bottle of soft drink. As soon as you open the bottle, gas bubbles out of the liquid. This gas is carbon dioxide.

Acid rain

One of the main causes of pollution in the modern world is acid rain. It is caused by a gas called sulfur dioxide, which is given off into the air when coal and other fuels burn. In the air, the gas dissolves in the water in raindrops to form an acid solution, so that when it rains, it rains acid. Acid rain can attack trees and kill life in streams and rivers.

▶ Stone columns and "icicles" form in the caves in limestone rock. They form when water drips from the roof to the floor of the cave. The water contains dissolved lime. When some of the water evaporates from each drip, tiny specks of lime are deposited. These specks build up into these columns and "icicles".

Q What are the proper names of these stone columns and "icicles"?

22

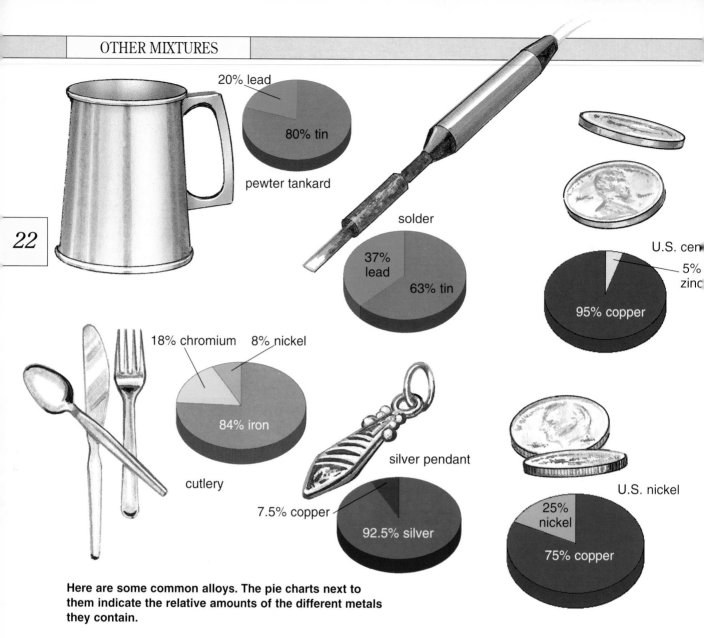

20% lead

80% tin

pewter tankard

solder

37% lead

63% tin

U.S. cent

5% zinc

95% copper

18% chromium   8% nickel

84% iron

cutlery

silver pendant

7.5% copper

92.5% silver

25% nickel

75% copper

U.S. nickel

Here are some common alloys. The pie charts next to them indicate the relative amounts of the different metals they contain.

Other mixtures

Solutions, as we have seen, consist of solids and liquids whose particles are thoroughly mixed together in the liquid state. Another important class of mixture is what is called the solid solution. This consists of a mixture of solids, whose particles are thoroughly mixed together.

The metal materials we call alloys are solid solutions. They consist of a mixture of different metals. They are made by melting the metals so that they dissolve in one another to form a liquid solution. This solution becomes solid when it cools.

Improving the properties

We mix metals together to form alloys for a good reason. Most pure metals are relatively soft and weak, but when certain amounts of other metals are added to them, they become much stronger and harder.

Metals are also added to one another to improve other properties. Iron by itself rusts easily, but if you add chromium and nickel to it, it rusts no longer. It becomes stainless steel.

More mixtures

Mixtures are all around us in the natural world too. Most rocks, for example, are made up of a mixture of minerals. You can see the different colored specks of minerals in most rocks. Soil is a mixture of many things, from ground-up bits of rock to the bodies of dead insects.

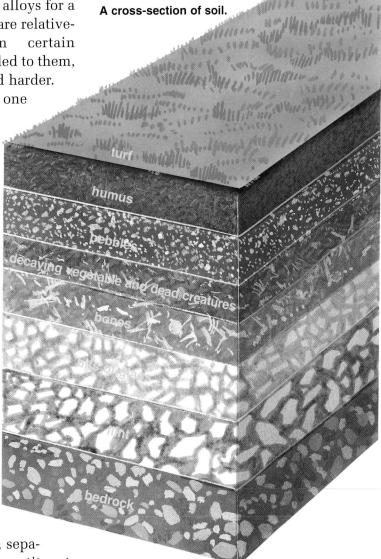

A cross-section of soil.

turf

humus

pebbles

decaying vegetable and dead creatures

bones

bits of organic

flint

bedrock

23

Separating mixtures

You could, if you were patient, separate out by hand the various constituents that make up a sample of soil. You might end up with a pile of stones, a few sticks, some dead worms, and bits of glass.

Separating a mixture by hand is sometimes not possible, so we must use other methods. Filtering is one method. We use it, for example, to separate the grounds from the solution when we prepare filter coffee. To separate the lumps in flour, we use a sieve. In general we can separate the various ingredients in a mixture by making use of differences in their properties.

Q **1.** You are given a mixture of iron filings and sugar. How can you separate them?

Q **2.** You are given a mixture of salt and very fine sand. How can you separate them?

2
Elements and Atoms

◀ **In an explosion, chemical reactions take place very rapidly. The chemical elements in the explosive rearrange themselves to create gases, and great heat is given out.**

Q Can you explain how such reactions can cause an explosion?

▼ **Both Democritus and Dalton thought that atoms were like little round balls. They were the smallest particles of matter that could exist. You couldn't have half an atom, for example. The word "atom" comes from a Greek word meaning "that which cannot be divided".**

Matter in one form or another is all around us. Exactly what is matter and what is it made of? Today, scientists tell us that matter is made up of substances called the chemical elements, combined together in different ways.

Scientists began to realize that the elements were the building blocks of matter in the early 1800s. Before then, people were quite mystified about what matter was like. Many still held the ancient Greek view that matter was composed of different proportions of just four elements — earth, air, fire, and water.

One ancient Greek philosopher named Democritus put forward a different view of matter. He said that different kinds of matter were made up of different arrangements of tiny invisible balls, which he called atoms. Democritus's atomic view didn't catch on.

An English chemist, John Dalton, put forward a similar idea in the early 1800s. As a result of chemical experiments, he said that matter is made up of atoms, and that the different chemical elements are made up of different atoms. This is what we believe today.

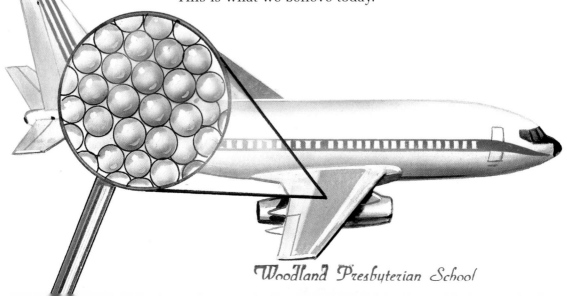

The chemical elements

In our world, we find literally thousands and thousands of different kinds of materials — limestone rock, aluminum, wood, flesh, water, and air. All these materials appear quite different from one another and from the many thousands of other materials. Our material world, then, looks very complicated.

Let's probe a little deeper. Suppose you are a skilled chemist and can analyze, or study the make-up of, all these different materials. What do you find?

When you analyze limestone rock, for example, you find it is made up of three basic substances combined together – calcium, carbon, and oxygen. You can't break down these substances any further.

You can't break down aluminum into simpler substances at all. It is itself a basic substance. You can break down wood into three basic substances – carbon, hydrogen, and oxygen. You can break down water into two – hydrogen and oxygen.

▲ A star blasts itself apart in a supernova explosion. Astronomers think that most of the elements that now make up the Earth were created in a supernova explosion of a massive star long ago.

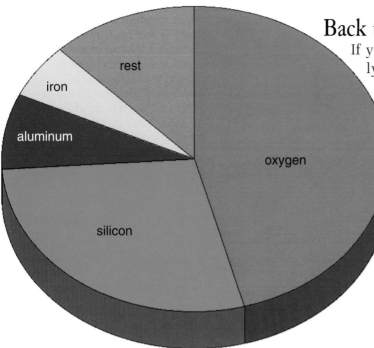

Back to basics

If you were superhuman and could analyze every other material, you would find that, in all the world, there are only about 92 basic substances.

Every kind of material that exists is made up of one or more of these 92 substances combined together. We call them the chemical elements. They are the basic building blocks of matter, not only on Earth, but also in the Universe as a whole.

WORKOUT

The pie chart above shows the relative amounts of the main elements in the Earth's crust. By measurement, express the amounts as percentages.

◀ This gleaming water tower in Merritt Island, Florida, is constructed of aluminum alloy. Aluminum is a metallic element, or metal. Most of the elements are metals. Aluminum is widely used in construction work because it is light but strong, and it doesn't corrode, or rust away.

▶ The leopard is one of the most beautiful creatures in the animal world. It is composed largely of three elements combined together – carbon, hydrogen, and oxygen. These elements are non-metals. They are the main elements in all living things.

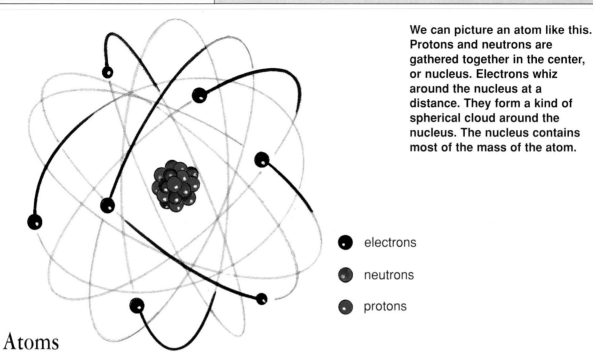

We can picture an atom like this. Protons and neutrons are gathered together in the center, or nucleus. Electrons whiz around the nucleus at a distance. They form a kind of spherical cloud around the nucleus. The nucleus contains most of the mass of the atom.

28

electrons

neutrons

protons

Atoms

As we saw earlier, all the substances we find in the natural world are made up of about 92 chemical elements. The smallest particles of these elements are atoms. Each element has a different atom.

As a result of experiments at the end of the 19th century and early in the 20th century, scientists found that atoms are themselves made up of still smaller particles. We call them subatomic particles because they are smaller than the atom.

The main subatomic particles are protons, neutrons, and electrons. Protons and neutrons are about the same size, but electrons are nearly 2,000 times smaller. Protons and electrons are electrically charged, but neutrons have no charge. Protons have a positive charge, and electrons a negative charge.

Q How do you think neutrons got their name?

Atomic structure

The atoms of the different elements are made up of different numbers of the three subatomic particles. They all have the same basic structure, pictured in the illustration opposite.

The simplest atom of all is hydrogen. It has only one proton in the nucleus, and only one electron circling around. The electron travels around the nucleus, not in a constant

IT'S AMAZING!

It would take over 4,000 trillion trillion protons to weigh 1 ounce (150 trillion trillion protons to weigh 1 gram)!

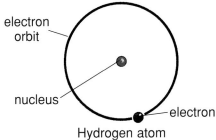

electron orbit

nucleus

electron

Hydrogen atom

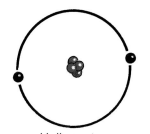

Helium atom

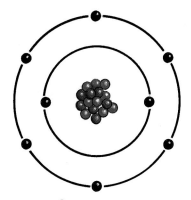

Oxygen atom

path, but in an ever-changing path, always staying the same distance from the nucleus. You can imagine the nucleus being surrounded by a shell, and the electron whizzing around in all directions on the inside of this shell. In fact, scientists do call the region where the electron can be found an electronic shell.

The next simplest atom after hydrogen is helium. This has two protons and two neutrons in the nucleus, and two electrons whizzing around in the electronic shell. Next comes lithium, with three protons and four neutrons in the nucleus and three electrons orbiting around it. Two are in the same shell that helium has. The third is in another shell farther out.

The atoms of the other elements are built up in the same way. They have extra protons and neutrons in the nucleus and extra electrons in shells at different distances around it.

The number of protons in the nucleus of the atoms of an element is called its atomic number.

In an atom, there is always the same number of electrons circling around the nucleus as there are protons in the nucleus.

Q Look again at the last sentence. What can we say about the electrical state of the atom as a whole?

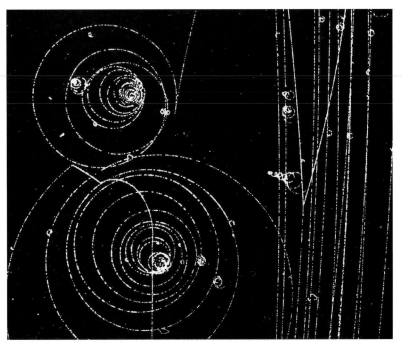

▶ Scientists produce subatomic particles in giant machines called atom-smashers. They can detect and identify the particles by the tracks they leave behind in particle detectors.

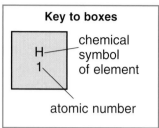

Key to boxes

chemical
symbol
of element

H
1

atomic number

The periodic table

All the elements have different atoms and different properties, but some elements have similar properties and behave in a similar way to others. They form kinds of chemical families.

Scientists have found a way of displaying the elements in their order to show the chemical family relationships. The arrangement is called the Periodic Table. In the table, the elements are listed in the order of their atomic number – the number of protons in the nucleus of their atoms.

The table is arranged into horizontal rows, called periods, and vertical columns, called groups. The elements in each group show the closest family relationships.

If you were superhuman and could analyze every other material that exists in nature, you would find that, in all the world, there are only 92 basic substances.

Every kind of natural material is made up of one or more of these substances combined together. We call them the chemical elements. They are the basic building blocks of matter, not only on Earth, but also in the Universe as a whole.

Group

Period

1	2								
H 1									
Li 3	Be 4								
Na 11	Mg 12								
K 19	Ca 20	Sc 21	Ti 22	V 23	Cr 24	Mn 25	Fe 26	Co 27	Ni 28
Rb 37	Sr 38	Y 39	Zr 40	Nb 41	Mo 42	Tc 43	Ru 44	Rh 45	Pd 46
Cs 55	Ba 56	La 57	Hf 72	Ta 73	W 74	Re 45	Os 76	Ir 77	Pt 78
Fr 87	Ra 88	Ac 39	Ku 104	Ha 105	106	107	108	109	

Periods are numbered 1–7 down the left side.

Lanthanides

Ce 58	Pr 59	Nd 60	Pm 61	Sm 62	Eu 63

6

Actinides

Th 90	Pa 91	U 92	Np 93	Pu 94	Am 95

7

The elements called the lanthanides are very similar indeed to lanthanum (La), and are included with it in a single block in the Table. Also, the elements called the actinides are very similar to actinium (Ac), and are included with it in a single block.

In addition to the natural elements, scientists have also made a number of artificial elements, bringing the total of elements known to more than 110.

Features of the table

Reactive metals: These elements are light metals that combine readily with other elements.
Transition metals: These elements are the typical metals – hard, dense, shiny, and strong.
Poor metals: These elements are metals that are softer and weaker than transition metals.

Semimetals: Also called metalloids; these elements have some properties of metals and some of non-metals.
Non-metals: These elements are not shiny, do not conduct electricity or heat, and are weak.
Noble gases: These elements combine hardly at all with the other elements.
Artificial elements: These elements do not exist in nature, but have been made by scientists.

31

Color Key

noble gases

non metals

semi metals

poor metals

Transition metals

artificial elements

reactive metals

Group

	3	4	5	6	7	0	Period
						He 2	1
	B 5	C 6	N 7	O 8	F 9	Ne 10	2
	Al 13	Si 14	P 15	S 16	Cl 17	Ar 18	3
Cu 29	Zn 30	Ga 31	Ge 32	As 33	Se 34	Br 35	Kr 36	4
Ag 47	Cd 48	In 49	Sn 50	Sb 51	Te 52	I 53	Xe 54	5
Au 79	Hg 80	Tl 81	Pb 82	Bi 83	Po 84	At 85	Rn 86	6

Period

									Period
Gd 64	Tb 65	Dy 66	Ho 67	Er 88	Tm 69	Yb 70	Lu 71		6
Cm 96	Bk 97	Ci 98	Es 99	Fm 100	Md 101	No 102	Lr 103		7

Period

Li 3	Be 4	Reactive metals
Na 11	Mg 12	
K 19	Ca 20	
Rb 37	Sr 38	
Cs 55	Ba 56	
Fr 87	Ra 88	

F 9	Halogens
Cl 17	
Br 35	
I 53	

Chemical families

In the Periodic Table, the closest family relationships can be seen in the groups on the left and right, that is, Groups 1 and 2, and Groups 7 and 0.

Groups 1 and 2 form the block of elements known as the reactive metals. These elements are light metals that are very reactive – they combine readily with other elements.

The halogens

The elements in Group 7 – fluorine, chlorine, bromine, and iodine – form another closely related family. They are called halogens and they are very reactive. Fluorine and chlorine, a poisonous gas. They will combine with many other elements. Chlorine combines with sodium to form sodium chloride, a very common chemical – table salt.

Q 1. Where do we find most sodium chloride?

Bromine is not a gas, but a brown fuming liquid. It is only one of two elements that is liquid at ordinary temperature. Iodine is a soft solid. We know it best in the form of a solution.

Q 2. Which is the other element that is liquid at room temperatures?

▶ **The color in fireworks comes from compounds of metals from Group 2, such as calcium, strontium, and barium.**

He 2	Noble gases
Ne 10	
Ar 18	
Kr 36	
Xe 54	
Rn 86	

The noble gases

The elements in Group 0 are all colorless and odorless gases. They are unlike any of the other elements. They react hardly at all with any other elements. That is why they are called the noble gases. They are sometimes called the inert gases.

The first gas in the Group, helium, is the lightest gas there is, apart from hydrogen. It is often used to provide the "lift" in balloons and airships.

Q Hydrogen is a lighter gas than helium and is cheaper to make. Why is helium used instead of hydrogen in balloons and airships?

▼ **When electricity is passed through neon gas, the gas glows a bright orange yellow. This is why neon lamps are widely used in advertising displays.**

Chemical Compounds

We can find a few of the elements in their pure state in the world around us. For example, we can find specks of gold and silver in the rocks and in the beds of streams. We call elements that we can find in their pure state, native elements.

We find most of the elements combined with other elements – as chemical compounds. We don't find pure iron in the rocks. We find iron usually in the form of a chemical compound in which it is combined with oxygen. Also, we don't find sodium or chlorine in the pure state. We find them combined together in the chemical compound we call table salt.

Q 1. Why do you think we can find gold but can't find sodium in its pure state in the ground?

Combinations

Table salt, as we have mentioned, is made up of the elements sodium and chlorine. It is not a mixture of these elements. We can usually separate the ingredients in a mixture quite easily, for example, by filtering (see page 23). But there is no easy way of separating the sodium from the chlorine in salt. That is because they are chemically bound together.

▲ **Gold jewelry and works of art keep their beauty and color for ever.**

▼ **Diamond is one of the uncombined, or native forms of carbon. Another is graphite.**

Q 2. What is the main difference between diamond and graphite?

▶ **Anthracite (a high-grade coal) is one of our best fuels – it is nearly pure carbon.**

Q 3. What is the name of the gas formed when anthracite burns?

When fuels burn, the substances they are made of (usually carbon and hydrogen) combine with the oxygen of the air to form gases. Again, you can't easily separate the combined elements in the gases because they are combined chemically.

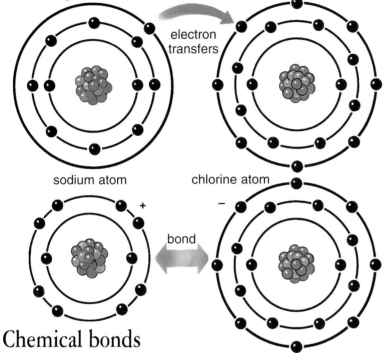

electron transfers

sodium atom

chlorine atom

bond

◀ When a sodium atom combines with a chlorine atom, an electron is transferred between them.

◀ In the compound sodium chloride, the sodium atom ends up with one less electron, and the chlorine atom with one more.

Chemical bonds

Almost all the elements combine with several other elements to form thousands upon thousands of different compounds. The elements in a compound are joined together by chemical links, called bonds. The bonds are made by electrons, usually the electrons in the outer shells of the combining atoms (see page 29).

There are two main kinds of bonds. In one kind, atoms share their electrons. In the other, atoms give and take electrons, as they do in the compound sodium chloride.

When a sodium atom combines with a chlorine atom, it gives up an electron. The chlorine atom takes in this electron. Because the electron has a negative electric charge, the chlorine atom ends up with a negative charge. Because the sodium atom has lost an electron, it ends up with a positive charge. So in the compound sodium chloride, bonds are formed between charged atoms.

Q What kind of forces do you think holds the charged atoms together?

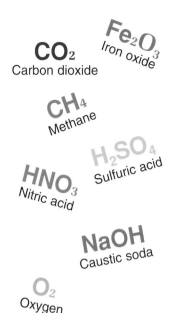

CO_2
Carbon dioxide

Fe_2O_3
Iron oxide

CH_4
Methane

H_2SO_4
Sulfuric acid

HNO_3
Nitric acid

$NaOH$
Caustic soda

O_2
Oxygen

Chemical Formulas

We have seen earlier that an atom of sodium and an atom of chlorine bond together to form a chemical compound called sodium chloride (table salt). The name of this chemical tells you which elements combined to make it. Chemists use a shorthand method of writing sodium chloride, using the chemical symbols of the elements: Na for sodium and Cl for chlorine. They write sodium chloride as NaCl. This is called the chemical formula of sodium chloride.

In a similar way, we have seen how an atom of carbon bonds with two atoms of oxygen to form a molecule of carbon dioxide. Using the chemical symbols of these elements, the chemical formula of carbon dioxide is CO_2. The 2 tells you that in each molecule of carbon dioxide, one atom of carbon combines with two atoms of oxygen.

Reactions and equations

Chemical reactions are taking place all around us – and inside us – all the time. One of the most common chemical reactions is burning. Wood burns in bonfires, gasoline burns in car engines, and gas burns in a kitchen stove.

▶ A rusting iron hull of a boat. The rusting of iron is a common chemical reaction. It takes place when iron is exposed to damp air. To prevent iron from rusting, it must be protected from the air, by painting, for example.

In each case, the fuel reacts (combines chemically) with the oxygen of the air. During the reaction, heat is given out. Heat is given out in many chemical reactions. In others, heat is taken in.

Most fuels consist of compounds containing hydrogen and carbon. When fuels burn, both the hydrogen and the carbon combine with oxygen. Carbon, for example, combines with oxygen to form carbon dioxide. We can write this reaction in the following way, where the + sign means "reacts with" and the ➜ sign means "to produce."

carbon + oxygen ➜ carbon dioxide

This way of representing the reaction is called a word equation.

We can also write this equation in a shorter form, using the chemical formulas of the substances taking part in the reaction: $C + O ➜ CO_2$

This equation is not quite accurate, though. For one thing, we know that two oxygen atoms are combined with the carbon atom in a molecule of carbon dioxide. For another, single oxygen atoms do not exist by themselves in the air. Oxygen gas is made up of oxygen molecules containing two atoms of oxygen, which we represent by O_2.

The correct equation for the reaction of carbon with oxygen to produce carbon dioxide is: $C + O_2 ➜ CO_2$

Summing up, when we write a chemical equation to represent a reaction, the number of atoms on each side of the equation must balance. From a balanced equation, chemists can work out the relative amounts of the substances that will react together.

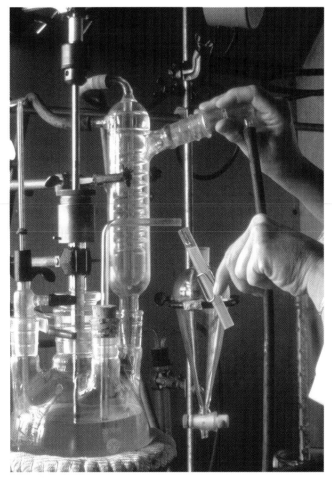

▶ Chemists carry out all kinds of chemical reactions in the laboratory. They use reactions to try to analyze substances, that is, find out what compounds or elements they contain. They also use reactions to try to synthesize, or make, new substances.

38

Acids, Bases, and Salts

Among the most common kinds of chemicals are the substances we call acids. When you drink lemon juice, the substance that makes it taste very sour is an acid. It is citric acid. Oranges, grapefruits, and limes also contain this acid, which is why they and lemons are called citrus fruits.

Another familiar acid substance is vinegar. It is a weak solution of acetic acid (also called ethanoic acid). As you know, this also tastes sour. In fact all acids taste sour.

Citric acid is unpleasant to taste because it is so sour, but it won't harm you. We call it a weak acid. Some of the other acids are poisonous and are dangerous to handle. We call them strong acids. One of the most common strong acids is sulfuric acid. When it is concentrated (very strong), it will burn flesh and char paper.

▲ Citrus fruits taste sour because of the acid they contain.

Alkalis

The chemical opposites of acids are also relatively common. After you have eaten certain foods, you might get an acid stomach. This means that the stomach has produced too much acid and this is making you feel uncomfortable. What you do is take an antacid, such as milk of magnesia. Milk of magnesia is the chemical substance magnesium hydroxide. It is a class of chemical called an alkali. Alkalis are the chemical opposites of acids. They combine with acids and neutralize them, or in other words, combat their acidity.

The acid that causes an acid stomach is called hydrochloric acid. When you swallow milk of magnesia, it combines with the hydrochloric acid in your stomach to form the chemical compound magnesium chloride. This compound is a class of chemical known as a salt. Salts are neither acid not alkaline – they are neutral.

In general when an acid reacts with an alkali, the products formed are a salt and water.

▶ A car battery contains a solution of sulfuric acid.

Strong alkalis

Magnesium is one of the reactive metals. The other reactive metals also form hydroxides that are alkalis. Sodium hydroxide is one of the strongest alkalis. Like the strong acids, it is poisonous and will burn flesh.

Q Can you remember what its popular name is?

39

INVESTIGATE

Cabbage indicator

You can make an indicator using red cabbage. Cut up the cabbage into small pieces. Boil some pure distilled or deionized water in a saucepan, then add the cabbage. Boil for a few minutes more, then let the saucepan cool. Next, pour the contents through a sieve, collecting the water in a jar. You can eat the cabbage as a vegetable.

The cabbage water is your indicator, which is ready for use. Use it to test the following: lemon juice, orange juice, bicarbonate of soda, sugar solution, salt solution, milk of magnesia medicine, baths salts, dissolved antacid tablet, vinegar. What color does your indicator turn in acid and alkaline solutions?

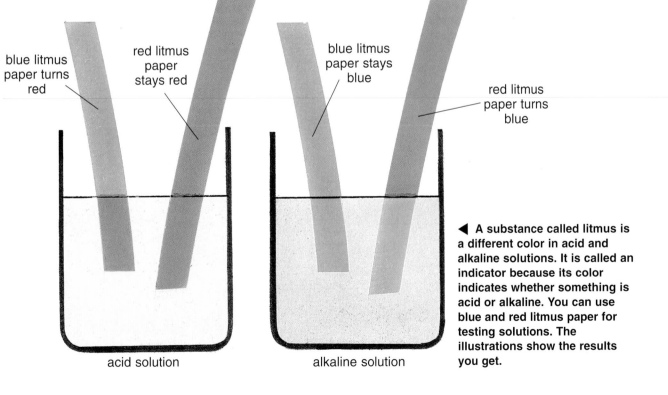

blue litmus paper turns red

red litmus paper stays red

blue litmus paper stays blue

red litmus paper turns blue

acid solution

alkaline solution

◀ **A substance called litmus is a different color in acid and alkaline solutions. It is called an indicator because its color indicates whether something is acid or alkaline. You can use blue and red litmus paper for testing solutions. The illustrations show the results you get.**

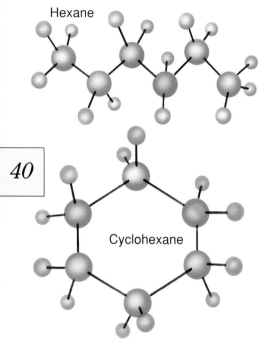

Hexane

Cyclohexane

40

Carbon Chemistry

Carbon is one of the most widespread of all the chemical elements. It is a native element, found in two very different forms in the rocks – as graphite and diamond. Carbon is also found combined with other elements in many minerals, for example chalk, which is calcium carbonate (formula, $CaCO_3$).

Carbon is unusual among the non-metal elements because it conducts electricity. It is unique among all the elements in the way its atoms can bond with one another to form long chains and rings. These form the "backbone" of large and often complicated molecules. The diagrams on the left show just two of the many thousands of different compounds carbon forms.

Carbon compounds are found most widely in living things. The bodies of living things are made up of carbon compounds, and reactions between carbon compounds produce the food and energy living things need to stay alive and grow.

The carbon cycle

Carbon circulates throughout the environment, a process called the carbon cycle. Plants take in carbon dioxide from the air to make their food, in a process called photosynthesis. In the process, they give off oxygen. When plant material dies and decays or is burned, carbon returns to the air as carbon dioxide. Animals take in carbon compounds by eating plants. They take in oxygen to "burn" their food inside them, and release carbon dioxide back into the air.

CO_2

CO_2

CO_2

O_2

plant

rotting vegetation

Organic chemicals

The study of carbon compounds forms one of the major divisions of chemistry, called organic ("living") chemistry. The study of all the other elements is called inorganic chemistry.

Chemists have used the unique property of carbon in forming long chains and rings to create a vast range of organic compounds. They include plastics, dyes, drugs, and pesticides. They use as their starting point natural supplies of organic chemicals, found in petroleum, coal, and natural gas. These fuels are made up of mixtures of compounds called hydrocarbons, in which carbon is combined with hydrogen.

Q Petroleum, coal, and natural gas are called fossil fuels. Why?

Refining the crude

Most organic chemicals are made these days from petroleum, and are known as petrochemicals. They are produced in an oil refinery. There, the petroleum, or crude oil, is processed to separate out the various hydrocarbons it contains.

The first main separating process is distillation, outlined in the diagram on the right. In this process, oil vapor is introduced into the column. The various hydrocarbons condense, or turn back into liquid, in one of the trays. They each have a different boiling point and condense in the tray kept at a temperature just below their boiling point.

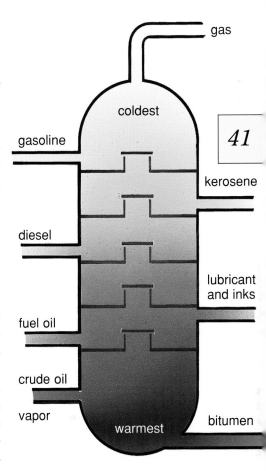

41

▲ **An outline of a distillation column at an oil refinery. Oil vapor is introduced into the column and the various substances in it condense in the various trays, according to their boiling point.**

A typical oil refinery installation.

3

Natural and Synthetic Materials

In the modern world, we use thousands of different materials to construct our buildings, build the machines we operate or travel in, and make our numerous appliances, gadgets, and devices.

In general, these materials have themselves been made by processing raw materials. Raw materials are materials such as minerals, which are found in the natural environment. We use some raw materials, however, in more or less the same state as we find them. Wood is a good example.

The most important of the mineral raw materials found in the rocks are those we call ores. These are the minerals from which we can extract metals. Other minerals are processed into a variety of products, from acids and fertilizers to cement and glass.

Our other major raw material is petroleum, or crude oil. At oil refineries, it is processed to give a wide range of organic chemicals. Products made from these chemicals are called synthetic materials. Plastics are the most common class of synthetics.

◀ **The huge nozzles of the first-stage engines of the mighty Saturn 5 Moon rocket. They were constructed from special metal alloys chosen because of their resistance to high temperatures. Even so, they had to be cooled to prevent them from melting when the rockets ignited.**

Forest products

Wood was one of the first raw materials our ancestors used, and it is still a valuable natural resource. Vast forests once covered North America and most other regions of the world, but over the last 300 years they have been cut down to clear the land for agriculture.

As in many developed parts of the world, foresters in North America treat trees as a crop. They try to plant as many trees as they cut down to insure a supply of lumber for future generations.

44

Softwoods and hardwoods

Different kinds of trees produce different kinds of wood. Conifer trees, such as firs and pines, produce relatively soft woods, and they are called softwoods. The oak, ash, and beech and other broad-leaf trees produce relatively hard wood, and so are called hardwoods.

Q What does "conifer" mean? What is the main difference between conifer trees and the hardwoods?

IT'S AMAZING!

An area of forest bigger than California has to be cut down each year to produce the wood pulp needed to make all the paper used in the world.

◀ Forestry in North America is a large and important industry. Lumberjacks now use powerful chain saws to fell the trees. The trees are trimmed, and then the trunks are removed by tractors.

Using wood

Wood is a very versatile material, with many uses. In some countries, it is used mainly as a fuel. In others it is used in building houses. Vast amounts of wood are also made into wood pulp and paper (see Box).

Wood pulp is also the starting point for a range of chemicals which are made into such products as plastics, fibers, and explosives. These chemicals are based on cellulose, the main chemical compound in wood.

Other manufactured wood products are also widely used. They include plywood. This is a kind of sandwich, made up of thin sheets of wood glued together. Particle board, or chipboard, is another product, made up of a pressed mixture of wood chips and resin.

45

Making paper

The first stage of papermaking is to convert solid wood into a pulpy mass. This takes place at a pulp mill. The logs taken from the forest can be converted into pulp in two ways. One, they can be shredded mechanically by means of rotating grindstones. Or they can be broken down by treatment with chemicals. Both methods convert the wood into a mass of coarse fibers known as wood pulp.

The pulp is usually transported to the paper mill in the form of dry sheets. At the mill, the sheets are mixed with water before being fed to a beater. In the beater, the coarse fibers are made finer and more flexible. Coloring matter and other materials may then be added with more water in a mixer. Then the water pulp is fed on to a moving belt on the papermaking machine. Water drains away, leaving a damp web of fibers. This passes through rollers and over drying cylinders, where it dries into paper sheet.

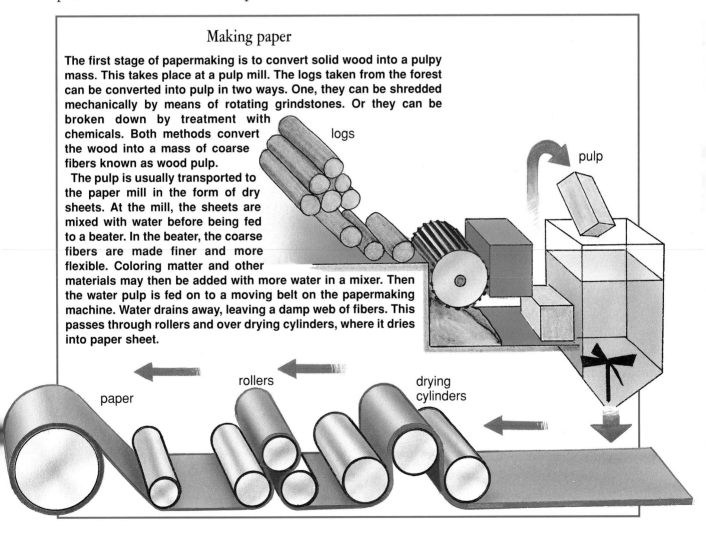

logs

pulp

paper

rollers

drying cylinders

46

◄ Glass is made by melting a mixture of sand, lime, and other materials in a furnace. Glassblowers shape their wares from molten glass. They give the initial shape to the glass by blowing into a blob of molten glass. They then add other pieces and manipulate them into shape by hand.

Rocks and minerals

North America has plentiful supplies of rocks and minerals, and mines vast amounts of them every year. Some of the mined materials are used as they are. For example, crushed stone, sand, and gravel are used in construction work and for making concrete. In the United States alone, more than two billion tons (1.8 billion tonnes) of these materials are extracted and used every year.

Most rock and mineral raw materials, however, are not useful until they have been processed in some way. Much sulfur, for example, is processed into sulfuric acid, one of the most widely used industrial chemicals. Phosphate rock for example is treated with sulfuric acid to make the fertilizer superphosphate.

Q Sulfur is an element and can be found by itself in the rocks. We can therefore say that sulfur is one of the .... elements. What is the missing word?

▶ Extracting ore at an open-pit mine. Many ores are worked from the surface in this way. If they are soft enough, they can be extracted simply by scooping them up with huge power shovels. Otherwise, explosives must be used first to break up the ore deposit.

Metals from minerals

The most useful of all the mineral raw materials are the ores. These are compounds of metals with other elements, from which the metals can be extracted.

Among the most important of all the ores are the iron ores, in which the iron is combined with oxygen. One of the richest iron ores is magnetite.

Q This ore has a unique property among ores. What do you think this could be?

Metal	Main ores
Aluminium	Bauxite
Copper	Azurite, chalcopyrite, cuprite, malachite
Gold	Native metal
Iron	Magnetite, hematite, limonite
Lead	Galena
Platinum	Native metal
Silver	Argentite, native metal
Tin	Cassiterite
Zinc	Blended

WORKOUT

About 100 million tons (90 million tonnes) of steel are made in the United States every year. Assuming the steel furnaces are run continuously, everyday throughout the year, how much steel is produced every hour? Give your answer to the nearest thousand tons.

Smelting metals

As mentioned earlier, the iron ores are very important because we extract iron – our most useful metal – from them. Iron is not used widely in the pure state. It is used most in the form of an alloy – the metal we call steel. Steel is iron mixed with a little carbon, and usually with other metals as well. The United States alone produces about 100 million tons of steel a year.

The blast furnace

Iron is extracted from the iron ore in a blast furnace. The ore is heated fiercely in the furnace with coke (mainly carbon) and limestone. This heating process, called smelting, releases the iron from the ore. At the temperature of the furnace, the iron is molten and collects at the bottom. It is tapped off from time to time. The iron produced is usually

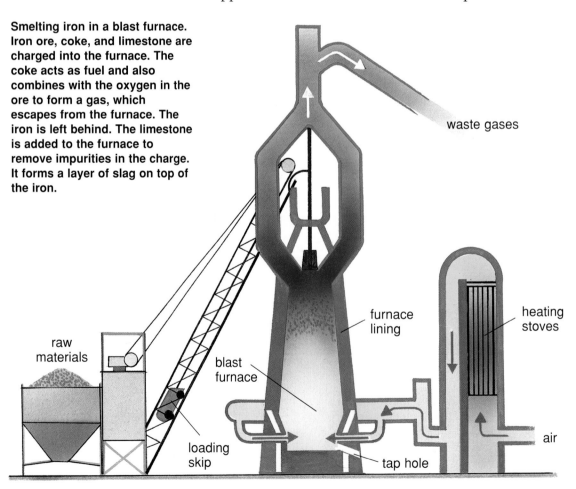

Smelting iron in a blast furnace. Iron ore, coke, and limestone are charged into the furnace. The coke acts as fuel and also combines with the oxygen in the ore to form a gas, which escapes from the furnace. The iron is left behind. The limestone is added to the furnace to remove impurities in the charge. It forms a layer of slag on top of the iron.

raw materials

waste gases

furnace lining

heating stoves

blast furnace

loading skip

tap hole

air

known as pig iron. It contains a lot of impurities, and must be refined, or purified, before it is ready for use.

Refining processes

The main impurity in pig iron is carbon. Most, but not all, of this must be removed to make steel. Today, most steel is made by the basic-oxygen process. In this process, molten pig iron is poured into a container called a converter. Then a jet of oxygen is directed into the converter at supersonic speed. The carbon and other impurities burn off, leaving a much purer metal – steel.

The best-quality steels are produced in a different way – by melting steel scrap in an electric furnace. The scrap is carefully selected so that the steel formed has the right composition.

Extracting other metals

Other metals besides iron are produced by smelting, including lead, zinc, and copper. Copper smelting produces an impure metal, which is refined using electrolysis.

Electrolysis is a process in which compounds are split up into their elements by means of electricity. The Investigation shows you how the process works.

INVESTIGATE

Copper capers

For this Investigation you need a 9-volt battery, some copper wire, a copper nail, a key, and some copper sulfate crystals. Dissolve some of the crystals in water to make a copper sulfate solution. Attach the wires to the key and nails as shown, and dip them into the solution. Connect the other ends of the wires to the battery, making sure you connect them to the correct terminals. Leave the experiment running for a while, then look at the key. What has happened to it? Leave the experiment running for a while longer, then look at the copper nail. What has happened to it?

battery

copper sulfate solution

◀ **A stage in copper smelting known as poling. A wooden pole is plunged into the impure molten copper. As the pole burns, it removes oxygen from the molten metal and helps purify it. After this process, the copper is 99 percent pure.**

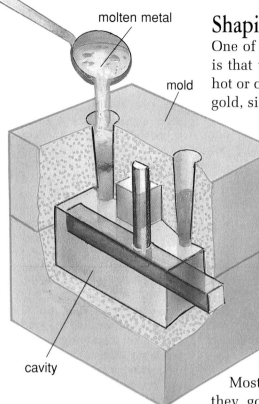

molten metal

mold

cavity

▲ **Molten metals can be cast into shape in molds. The molten metal is poured into a cavity made in special sand.**

Shaping metals

One of the properties of metals that makes them so useful is that they are easy to shape. They may be shaped when hot or cold. Among the metals that are easiest to shape are gold, silver, and copper.

Gold and silver, for example, can easily be hammered into shape when cold. We call them malleable metals. Copper can be easily drawn into fine wire when cold. We call it a ductile metal. The other metals are not as malleable or as ductile.

Metals may be shaped in a variety of different ways, including casting, rolling, forging, and pressing.

Casting is a method of shaping using molten metal. A mold of the required shape is made in firm sand, then molten metal is poured in. When the metal cools and hardens, it takes the shape of the mold.

Most metals are cast into ingots (blocks) or slabs before they go for further processing, such as rolling. In this method, a slab of metal is softened by reheating and is

▶ **Blacksmiths shape metal by forging. They hammer the hot metal into shape on an anvil.**

WORKOUT

Gold is the most malleable metal. lit can be hammered into very thin sheet, known as gold leaf.

Incredibly, 4 pounds of gold can be beaten into gold leaf with an area of 1,100 square yards. Gold has a density of about 1,200 lb./cu. ft. Work out the thickness of the gold leaf. Give your answer in inches. (In metric: 2 kg of gold can be beaten into leaf with an area of 1,020 square meters. Gold has a density of 19.3 g/cc. Give your answers in millimeters.)

▶ The body panels of a car are made from steel sheet. They are pressed into shape when cold on powerful hydraulic presses. Then they are welded together to form the car body.

passed through heavy rollers, which gradually reduce its thickness. The thin metal sheet produced may then be rolled cold.

Forging, or hammering, is another widely used shaping method. In a drop forge, a heavy ram hammers a piece of hot metal into a shaped mold, or die. In a forging press, the hot metal is squeezed into shape by a ram, operated by hydraulic (liquid) pressure. Thinner sections of cold metal may also be given their final shape by pressing on a hydraulic press.

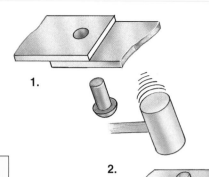

1.

2.

3.

▲ In riveting, pieces of metal are joined by headed rivets. They are inserted through holes in the metal, and then the tail end of the rivets are hammered to form a second head.

▶ Joining two lengths of pipeline by welding. The welder softens the edges of the two pipes by heating them with his welding torch, and then adds extra molten metal from a filler rod. A strong joint forms between the pipes when the metal cools.

Joining metals

Many metal objects can't be shaped in one operation. They have to be built by joining together a number of parts. Often metal parts are joined simply by nuts and bolts. Some are joined by riveting.

Welding is another common method of joining metals. It involves softening the edges of the metal parts to be joined and adding molten metal to the joint. Soldering is another joining method that uses a metal alloy called solder, which melts easily. The molten metal is dripped onto the joint and quickly sets. Soldering is used to join wires in electrical devices.

Q What do you think are the main advantages and disadvantages of joining parts by (A) nuts and bolts, and (B) welding?

52

Machining

After they have been shaped, many metal objects need further treatment. They may need holes drilled in them, for example. Or they may need polishing to make them look better, or grinding to bring them to exactly the right size and shape. Such metal-finishing processes are carried out by machine tools. They are driven by powerful electric motors and have hard cutting surfaces.

One of the most useful machine tools is the lathe. It carries out a machining process called turning. The lathe tools remove metal from a rotating workpiece (the piece of metal being worked on). Other common machine tools include the drill press and the milling machine. A drill press drills holes in the workpiece with a rotating bit. The milling machine cuts metal from the workpiece with a rotating cutting wheel.

Q On most machine tools, a liquid called a cutting oil is sprayed over the cutting area. What do you think is the purpose of doing this?

▲ Workers in industry and at home use power drills to bore holes in materials.

53

▼ The lathe is one of the most common kinds of machine tool. The shaft to be shaped is held between the headstock and tailstock, and rotated. A cutting tool attached to the tool post is moved in toward the shaft and peels off a ribbon of metal. Using the hand wheels, the lathe operator can move the cutting tool anywhere along the shaft very precisely.

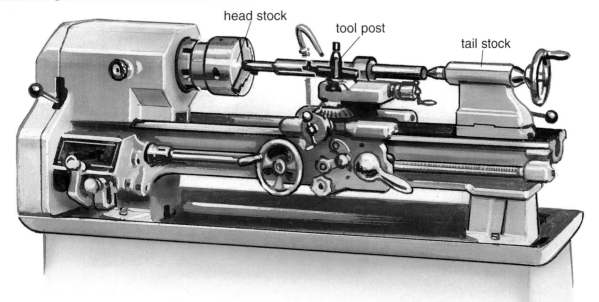

head stock   tool post   tail stock

54

Synthetics

Broadly speaking, we use the word synthetic to mean artificial or not natural. In this sense, most of the materials we use, including metals, are synthetic. However, the term is most often applied to products of the chemical industry that have been made from chemicals rather than from natural materials.

The main synthetic materials we use are those we call plastics. Most of them are made from petrochemicals – chemicals obtained by refining petroleum. The main features of plastics are that they have very large molecules and can be shaped easily.

One of the most common plastics is polyethylene. Like most other plastics, its large molecules have a "skeleton" made up of hundreds of carbon atoms joined together in a long chain. Among other common plastics are PVC (polyvinyl chloride), polystyrene, and nylon.

All these plastics are made by a process called polymerization. Each large molecule in the plastic is made by combining many small molecules of a certain chemical. For example, polyethylene is made by combining together many molecules of the gas ethylene. The product of polymerization is called a polymer.

mold   plastic tube

▶ **Blow molding is a method used to shape plastic containers. Hot plastic tubing is placed in a mold, and then air is blown in to force the plastic against the walls.**

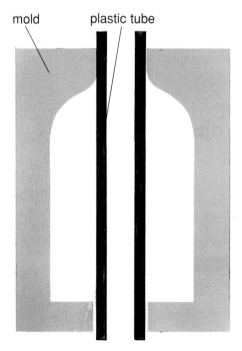

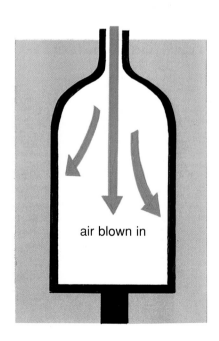

air blown in

Synthetic fibers

Nylon is a common plastic, but we know it better in the form of fibers. We use nylon fibers to make tights, socks, shirts, and many other textiles. Nylon was the first synthetic fiber, and is still one of the most important. Acrylic and polyester fibers are also widely used in fabrics. Like nylon, they are plastics that can easily be drawn out into fine fibers.

Composites

Some of the most useful plastics materials now being used are known as composites. They are a mixture of plastics with materials that give them added strength. One of the best-known composites is fiberglass. This is a tough and hard-wearing material made up of plastic reinforced (strengthened) with glass fibers. Another composite material uses carbon fibers to reinforce the plastic. Carbon-fiber materials are light but very strong and flexible. They are used to make tennis rackets, for example.

Plastics find hundreds of uses in and around the home. We even wear plastics, in the form of synthetic fibers.

56

4000 BC Copper was smelted from its ores and cast into molds in the Middle East.

400s BC The Greek philosopher Democritus put forward the idea that matter is made up of atoms.

AD 1200s The term alchemy came into use in Europe, relating to the practice of experimenting with chemicals in the hope, for example, of turning other metals into gold. Alchemy had been practiced in various parts of the world for over 1,000 years.

LATE 1700s French scientist Antoine Lavoisier carried out painstaking experiments investigating the nature of matter, and he is generally considered to be the father of chemistry.

1862 English chemist Alexander Parkes made the first plastic from cellulose nitrate and called it Parkesine.

1869 New Yorker John Hyatt made a similar cellulose nitrate plastic to Parkes, but marketed it more successfully, as celluloid.

1869 Russian chemist Dmitri Mendeleyev drew up his Periodic Table.

1897 English physicist J.J. Thomson discovered the electron.

1909 American chemist Leo Baekeland made the first synthetic plastic, bakelite.

1911 New Zealand physicist Ernest Rutherford discovered that atoms have a nucleus.

1931 American chemist Wallace Carothers headed a team that discovered neoprene synthetic rubber.

1932 American physicist Carl Anderson discovered the positron, the first particle of antimatter. Antimatter is made up of particles similar in some respects to particles of ordinary matter, but with a significant difference, for example, an opposite electric charge. The positron is the antiparticle of the electron, with a positive electric charge.

1935 American chemist Wallace Carothers headed a team that discovered the first synthetic fiber, nylon.

1940 American chemist Glenn Seaborg and co-workers E.M. McMillan, J.W. Kennedy, and A.C. Wahl made the first artificial element, plutonium.

1948 American physicists John Bardeen and William Brattain of Bell Telephone Laboratories developed semiconductor materials and invented the transistor.

1961 Scientists at Texas Instruments, in Texas, produced the silicon chip, containing many embedded electronic circuits.

1992 NASA scientists reported that the satellite COBE had provided evidence that the Universe began with a Big Bang about 15 billion years ago. All matter was created a short while after the Big Bang.

Glossary

ACID A common class of chemicals with a sour taste. An acid combines with a base to form a salt plus water.

ALKALI A base that dissolves in water.

ALLOY A metal mixture, containing one or more metals mixed together, or a mixture of a metal with another chemical element.

ATOM The smallest part of an element that can exist and still have the properties of that element.

ATOMIC NUMBER The number of protons in each atom of a particular element.

BOILING An action in which a liquid changes rapidly into a gas.

BONDING The means by which atoms join together.

CASTING A method of shaping molten metal in molds.

CERAMICS Materials made by baking clay or other earthy materials.

CHANGE OF STATE A change in the physical state of a substance, for example, from the solid state to the liquid state.

CHEMICAL ELEMENTS See ELEMENTS.

CHEMISTRY The study of the properties of the elements and their compounds.

COMPOSITE A synthetic material made up usually of a plastic reinforced (strengthened) by fibers. Fiberglass is a composite.

COMPOUND A substance made up of two or more elements combined together.

CONDENSATION The change in state when a gas turns back into a liquid.

CONDUCTOR A substance that conducts (passes on) heat and electricity well.

CONIFER A tree that produces its seeds in cones.

CORROSION A chemical process that attacks metals and causes them to break down. The rusting of iron is the most common form of corrosion.

CRYSTALS The regular shapes of minerals when they form.

DECIDUOUS TREE One that loses its leaves in the fall.

DIE A metal mold.

ELECTROLYSIS A process in which electricity is used to bring about a chemical change.

ELECTRON A tiny particle with a negative electric charge. Electrons circle around the nucleus of every atom.

ELEMENTS The chemical substances that are the basic building blocks of matter.

EVAPORATION The process of changing a liquid into a gas.

EVERGREEN TREE One that keeps its leaves through the winter.

EXTRUSION A shaping process for metals and plastics in which material is shaped by being forced through a die.

FORGING A metalworking process in which metal is hammered into shape.

GEM A mineral prized for its beauty.

HARDWOOD A hard wood obtained mainly from deciduous trees, such as the oak and beech, or tropical evergreen trees, such as teak and mahogany.

HYDRAULIC PRESS A metal-shaping machine that exerts its squeezing force by means of liquid pressure.

HYDROCARBON A compound made up of hydrogen and carbon only. Petroleum is made up mainly of a mixture of hydrocarbons.

INGOT A metal casting made immediately after a metal has been smelted.

KINETIC THEORY A theory that states that all matter is made up of particles in motion.

MACHINING A method of shaping metals using power-driven machine tools, such as lathes and drills.

MATTER The stuff from which the Universe is made.

MELTING The process of a solid changing into a liquid.

METAL An element that is typically hard and shiny and conducts heat and electricity well.

MINERAL A chemical compound found in the Earth's crust.

MOLDING A method of shaping materials in a mold, used with ceramics, metals, and plastics.

MOLECULE The smallest unit of a compound made up of two or more atoms combined together.

NATIVE ELEMENT An element found in its uncombined state in the Earth's crust.

NEUTRON A particle found in the nucleus of most atoms. It has much the same mass as a proton, but has no electric charge.

NOBLE GAS A gas that does not combine readily with other chemical substances. Neon is an example of a noble gas.

NUCLEUS The center part of an atom, in which most of the mass of the atom is concentrated. See also PROTON, NEUTRON.

ORE A mineral from which a metal can profitably be extracted.

OXIDATION A common chemical reaction that takes place when a substance combines with oxygen.

PERIODIC TABLE A table that arranges the elements in a manner that shows the chemical relationships between them.

PETROCHEMICALS Chemicals obtained by processing petroleum.

PETROLEUM Oil as it comes out of the ground; crude oil.

PLASTICS Synthetic materials with large molecules that are easy to shape.

PLYWOOD A processed wood made up of thin slices of wood glued together.

POLYMERS Another name for plastics. It refers to the fact that most plastics are made by a process (polymerization) in which many small molecules are combined to make big ones. The word "polymer" means "many parts".

PROTON A particle found in the nucleus of all atoms. It has a positive electric charge.

REFINING Purifying. Metals are refined by having impurities removed. Petroleum is refined by being split into various parts, or fractions, containing different hydrocarbons.

ROLLING Shaping metal by passing it between heavy rotating rollers.

RUBBER An elastic material obtained by processing the sap of rubber trees.

SALT A substance formed when an acid and a base combine. Table salt is the chemical sodium chloride.

SEMICONDUCTOR A substance that conducts electricity a little. Silicon and other semimetals are examples.

SMELTING A common method of extracting metal from ores, by heating them fiercely in a furnace with other materials.

SOFTWOOD A wood that is relatively soft, obtained mainly from conifer trees.

SOLDERING A method of joining metals with an easy melting, quick setting alloy, solder.

SYNTHETIC FIBERS Textile fibers made from plastic materials.

SYNTHETICS Materials made wholly from chemicals. They contrast with natural materials, such as wood.

THERMOPLASTICS Plastics that soften when they are reheated.

WELDING A method of joining pieces of metal by melting the edges in contact and often adding additional molten metal in between.

WOOD PULP Wood fibers made by breaking down solid wood mechanically or chemically.

59

For Further Reading

Cobb, Vicki.
Why Can't You Unscramble an Egg?
Dutton, New York. 1990.

Darling, David.
From Glasses to Gases: The Science of Matter.
Macmillan, New York. 1992

Mebane, Robert.
Metals.
Twenty-first Century Books, New York. 1995.

Mebane, Robert.
Plastics and Polymers.
Twenty-first Century Books, New York. 1995.

Mebane, Robert.
Salts and Solids.
Twenty-first Century Books, New York. 1995.

Morgan, Sally.
Materials.
Facts on File, New York. 1994.

Parramon.
The Elements.
Barron, Woodbury, New York. 1994.

Pomeroy, Johanna.
Matter: Locating Details.
Educational Activities, New York. 1988.

Time-Life Books Staff.
Structure of Matter.
Time-Life, New York. 1992.

Wilkins, Fred.
Matter.
Children's Press, Chicago. 1986.

Answers

Page 9
In orbit, the shuttle circles the Earth about once every 1½ hours. The astronauts see 16 sunrises and sunsets every 24 hours.

Page 11
Workout
It would take the scent particles 6.1 seconds to reach the male moth. It would take the male moth 14 minutes 36.6 seconds to fly to the female. The answer to the question is 14 minutes 42.7 seconds.

Page 13
1. The purpose of coating steel with zinc is to prevent the steel from rusting. The process of coating steel in this way is called galvanizing.
2. "Hexagonal" means having six sides.

Page 14
Electricity made by harnessing water power is called hydroelectricity ("water-electricity").

Page 15
Investigations
Water, cola, vinegar, milk, olive oil, corn oil, dishwashing liquid, barbeque sauce, motor oil, toatoe ketchup, molasses.

If you add a drop of dishwashing liquid to the water, the needle will sink because the liquid greatly reduces the surface tension.

Page 17
Investigation
No matter in what position you place the jars, the smoke will always travel from one into the other. This is because the gas particles in each jar quickly mix and knock the smoke particles everywhere until they fill both jars.

1. The missing word is "pressure".
2. By pumping, you are adding energy to the gas; that is, increasing the kinetic energy of its particles and therefore its temperature.
3. The sailboat is prevented from going faster by the drag, or resistance, of the water on the boat hull.

Page 18
Mercury is special because it is the only metal that is liquid at ordinary temperatures.

Page 19
Investigation
The temperature in the saucepan stays the same until all the ice has melted. The heat going into the saucepan is needed to make the solid ice change into liquid water. The heat taken in is called latent heat.

Page 20
You can't put out an oil fire with water. The blazing oil floats on top of the water, because oil is less dense than water.

Page 21
Investigation
You will find that you can add less salt and sugar to the ice-cold water and more to the warm water. Substances are more soluble in warmer water.

The stone columns are called stalagmites, and the stone "icicles" are called stalactites.

Page 23
1. You can use a magnet to separate the iron filings from the sugar because iron is magnetic.
2. To separate the sand from the salt, first add water to the mixture and stir. The salt dissolves in the water, but the sand doesn't. You can then use a filter to separate the sand. You can get back the salt by heating the salt solution that passes through the filter. The heat will evaporate the water, leaving solid salt.

Page 25
The reactions give out great heat, which causes the gases produced to expand rapidly. This creates a violent shock wave, or blast.

Page 27
Workout
From the pie chart, oxygen makes up 46 percent, silicon 28 percent, aluminum 8 percent, iron 6 percent, and the remaining elements 12 percent of the Earth's crust.

Page 28
Neutrons got their name because they are electrically neutral.

Page 29
The atom is electrically neutral.

Page 32
1. We would find most sodium chloride dissolved in the water of the oceans.
2. The other liquid element is mercury.

Page 33
Hydrogen forms an explosive mixture with air. Helium does not. It is an inert (unreactive) substance.

Page 34
1. Sodium is a very reactive substance, but gold isn't.
2. The main difference between diamond and graphite is that diamond is very hard, while graphite is very soft.
3. When anthracite (nearly pure carbon) burns in air, the gas formed is carbon dioxide.

Page 35
Electrical forces hold together the charged atoms in sodium chloride.

Page 39
The popular name for sodium hydroxide is lye.

Page 39
Investigation
The cabbage-water indicator turns red in acid solutions and blue or green in alkaline solutions.

Page 41
Petroleum, coal, and natural gas are called fossil fuels because they are the remains of organisms that lived long ago.

Page 44
"Conifer" means cone-bearer, because these trees bear their seeds in cones. Most conifer trees are evergreen, while most hardwood trees are deciduous – they drop their leaves in the fall.

Page 46
The missing word is "native".

Page 47
Magnetite is unique because it is magnetic, which gives magnetite its name.

Investigation
While the plaster is setting, you notice that it gets warm. This tells you that a chemical reaction is taking place, which is giving out heat.

Page 48
Workout
About 11,000 tons (9,000 tonnes) of steel are produced in the United States every hour.

Page 49
Investigation
When you look at the key, you will see that it is becoming coated with pure copper. When you look at the nail, you will see that it is being eaten away. This process is called electroplating. Impure copper is refined in a similar way. The impure copper takes the place of the nail, and a pure copper plate takes the place of the key.

Page 51
Workout
The thickness of the gold leaf is 0.000004 inch (0.0001 mm). (Work out the volume of gold, then divide it by the area. Watch your units!)

Page 52
Parts joined by nuts and bolts can be taken apart, but the nuts may work free accidentally. Welded joints are very strong, but the parts can't be easily taken apart.

Page 53
The purpose of the cutting oil is threefold. It cools and lubricates the cutting area, and also helps flush away the pieces of cut metal.

Index